Be Calm AND COLOR

CHANNEL YOUR ANXIETY INTO
A SOOTHING, CREATIVE ACTIVITY

chartwell books

Create calm and tranquility through coloring!

It can be difficult to find peace amid the stress and worries of everyday life. Creating intentional quiet moments during the day is important for cultivating a calm life and reducing stress. Coloring is a great way to take a moment for yourself and unwind.

Coloring provides many of the same benefits as mindfulness and meditation. It allows you to be present and focus on one task. Coloring relaxes your brain and can improve sleep, focus, and brain function. It's also helpful for reducing anxiety.

The over 120 beautiful and intricate templates included in this book will bring you hours of relaxation. You can use markers, gel pens, crayons, or anything else you wish. There is no wrong way to color and no rules.

Relax, be calm, and start coloring today.

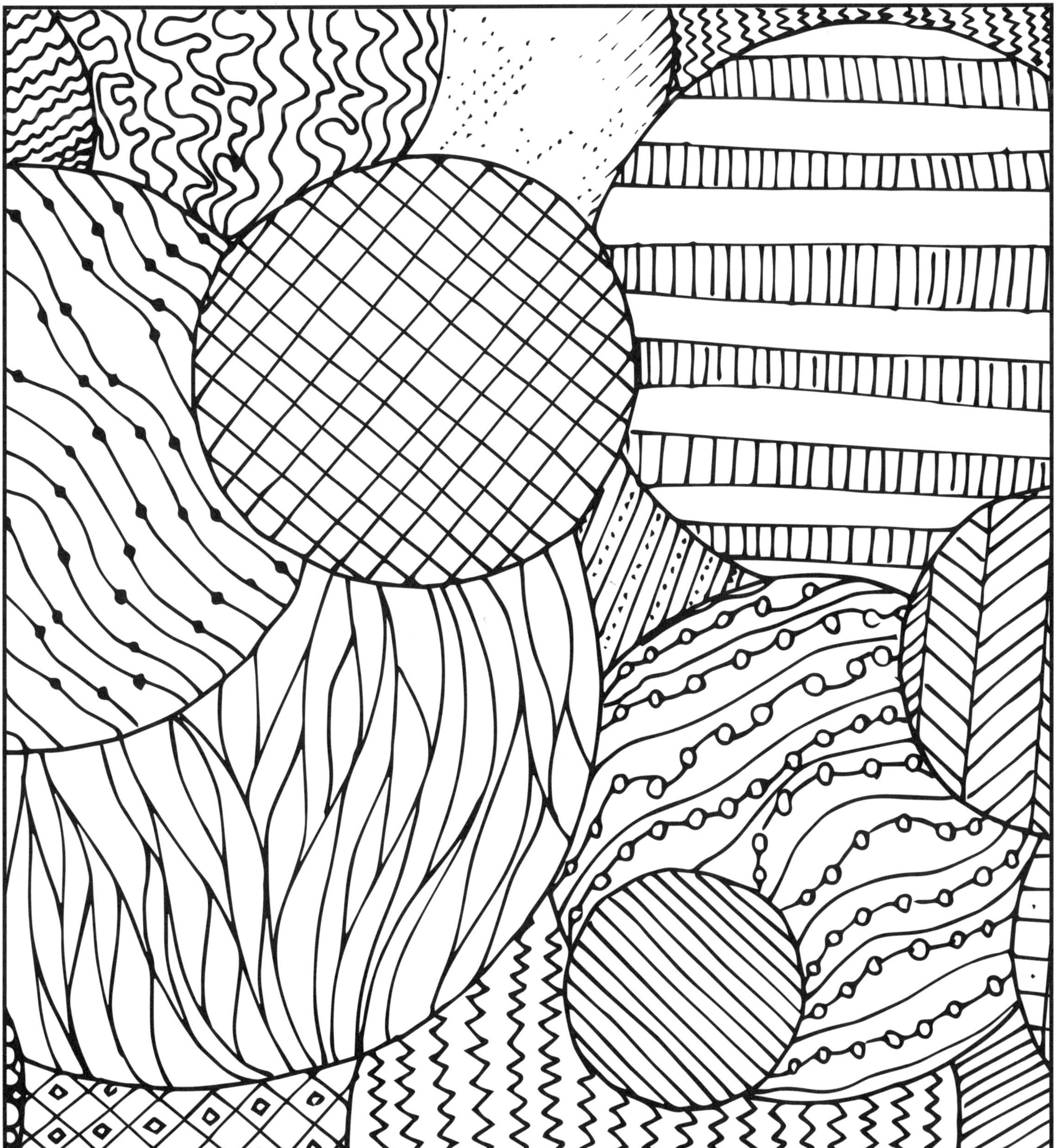

Quarto

This edition published in 2023 by Chartwell Books,
an imprint of The Quarto Group
142 West 36th Street, 4th Floor
New York, NY 10018 USA
T (212) 779-4972 F (212) 779-6058
www.Quarto.com

10 9 8 7 6 5 4 3 2 1

Chartwell titles are also available at discount for retail, wholesale, promotional, and bulk purchase. For details, contact the Special Sales Manager by email at specialsales@quarto.com or by mail at The Quarto Group, Attn: Special Sales Manager, 100 Cummings Center Suite 265D, Beverly, MA 01915, USA.

ISBN: 978-0-7858-4285-9

Publisher: Wendy Friedman
Senior Managing Editor: Meredith Mennitt
Senior Design Manager: Michael Caputo
Designers: Sue Boylan and Alana Ward
Editor: Cathy Davis
Image credits: Shutterstock